UP IN THE
AIR

WITH SHELLEY BERMAN

UP IN THE AIR

WITH SHELLEY BERMAN

Illustrations by Ed Powers

PRICE/STERN/SLOAN
Publishers, Inc., Los Angeles
1986

Special thanks to the McDonnell Douglas Corporation for supplying photographs for use in the preparation of artwork for this book.

TABLE OF CONTENTS

INTRODUCTION or HOW I CAME TO WRITE A BOOK ABOUT AIRLINES

People tend to think humorists view all their personal experiences as potential, if not immediate, jokes. One of the biggest laughs I ever got was when I was almost decapitated by the doors while getting into an elevator. My admirers laughed all the way from the eighteenth floor down to the lobby.

One day I was buying a lockback folding knife for fishing. The blade on this knife can't fold on you unless you press a hard spring. I was checking out the action when the sharp blade dropped unexpectedly, cutting the back of two of my fingers. The cuts were not serious but the bleeding was awful. I asked the shop owner to get me some bandages, which he did. As I worked covering my painful, bleeding fingers, the shop owner laughed and said, "Oh, I bet we're gonna have a routine out of this one, ha ha." Fortunately for both of us, the knife was closed.

While I do draw from life, I do not draw from individual incidents. I am not merely a kvetch, I am a professional kvetch; I want my complaints to have some lasting effect. My work is most often the result of years of intensive annoyance. And I never know exactly what will cause me to sit down and do something about it.

One day I took a flight on my favorite airline. The airline had just gone back into operation after settling its annual employees' strike. Since the strike had been a protracted one, the airline was offering very generous rebates to lure back its old customers. Even without the rebate I'd have chosen this line, and flown first class. I hate flying. I find it's worth paying the extra amount — what a difference! — since the luxury in first class makes flying substantially more tolerable for me. I looked forward to this flight in particular since it would be on a 747 and first class on a 747 offers a spaciousness that all but makes me forget I'm on a plane.

I said, "Non-smoking, aisle. Window-aisle." The friendly lady ticked her computer, marked my boarding pass, handed it to me with a friendly smile. I boarded the plane and was promptly shunted upstairs to what used to be the lounge. Low ceiling. Yes, First Class. Yes, window-aisle. No, not what I had been allowed to anticipate. Visions of comforting amplitude gone, I asked to speak to someone in authority. A friendly, uniformed man came on. I said I should have been told I'd be sitting in the attic — should have been granted the right to accept or reject. He said I asked for a window-aisle seat and that's what I got. I said no, this was an *upstairs* window-aisle seat; I had not asked for an *upstairs* window-aisle seat. He gave me a friendly smile and said, "That's your interpretation, sir." He bid me a friendly adieu and left.

I was seething. As the plane took off a man seated behind me said, "Looks like you've got a new routine there, Shel." Something suddenly felt weird. It was my face. I was smiling. I turned to him. "No, I've already done an airline routine. Years ago. This time, maybe a book."

Shelley Berman
Bell Canyon, California

9

"What are you up in the air about?"

"I'm worried because I don't feel guilty. I didn't wipe the sink with my towel as a courtesy to the next passenger. I thought, the hell with them! Nobody ever wipes the sink for me! I walked out of that lavatory leaving a filthy, soaking wet sink and I felt just great."

THE OVERHEAD COMPARTMENT

or GOVERNMENT REGULATIONS REQUIRE THAT YOU TAKE THIS BAG AND SHOVE IT

Examine this picture. Tom, Don and Mac, strangers to each other, are flying in peace under a single overhead compartment. But something is wrong. What is it?

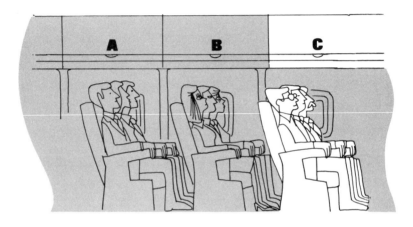

Figure #1

What is wrong is the overhead compartment, though directly over the heads of Tom, Don and Mac, is not for their exclusive use. It is not part of the package, like their seats or the complimentary beverage.

Proximity has nothing to do with determining whose overhead compartment is whose. The compartment just over your seat allows you merely the small advantage of getting to it first, if you're fast.

When it comes to staking a claim on an overhead compartment, speed and aggressiveness are everything. Tom, Don and Mac may or may not have stowed their things in the compartment just above them. Just because a compartment is directly overhead it does not follow that it belongs to the people seated directly underhead.

In fact, if your head mattered at all in determining overhead compartment possession, you might find the matter far more complicated than you dream. Take a look at Figure #2.

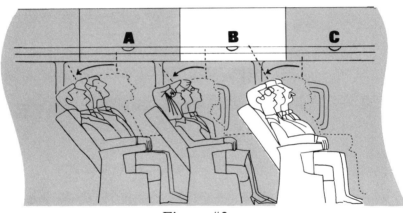

Figure #2

Figure #2 tells us two things. First, when flying, it is a mistake to use your head. Second, if proximity counts at all, six passengers may lay claim to one overhead compartment — compartment "B." See Figure #3.

Q. What is wrong with this picture?

A. Wow! *The center section has no overhead compartments!* Plus! We already know that the three people behind Tom, Don and Mac may lay equal claim to overhead compartment "B." Plus! What about Hal and Fay? Right now it looks like a total of eight people may lay claim to this one compartment!

In most planes with a center section of seats there are no overhead compartments to accommodate the passengers seated there. To these passengers overhead compartments are fair game, and rightly so. They push all they can under the seats in front of them, but in the end they all look like bag ladies. Otherwise decent, God-fearing Americans are forced to be overhead compartment parasites.

Q. What does it mean when the Flight Attendant says, "Government regulations require that all carry-on baggage be stowed safely under the seat in front of you or be placed in the overhead compartments provided for that purpose"?

A. It means, "Put those carry-ons away and we mean it! We've given you space to put that stuff, so if it doesn't seem to fit, shove it!"

Q. What if you're an impoverished young cellist with your instrument, going to an audition with the New York Philharmonic?

A. Shove it.

Q. Why do passengers seem to want to carry on all they can? Aren't airlines very careful about baggage which is checked through?

A. Extremely careful. Not only are airlines careful with checked baggage, they even have a special department for handling passenger claims for lost or damaged baggage.

"What are you up in the air about?"

"Ever try covering yourself with an airline blanket? You can cover yourself from your shoulders down to your waist, or from your waist down to your knees. Hell of a choice. You gotta decide whether you prefer a chest cold or frostbitten genitals!"

Q. Why do they tell you to check in at the gate a half-hour before departure time?

A. It's for your own good. The sooner you check in, the sooner you will find out about the delay.

FEAR OF FLYING
or THE CURSE OF COMMON SENSE

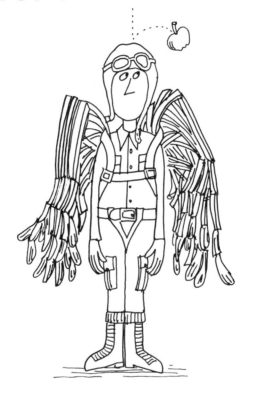

EVERY BODY CONTINUES IN ITS STATE OF REST, OR OF UNIFORM MOTION IN A RIGHT LINE, UNLESS IT IS COMPELLED TO CHANGE THAT STATE BY FORCES IMPRESSED UPON IT.

Projectiles continue in their motions, so far as they are not retarded by the resistance of the air, or impelled downwards by the force of gravity.

—*Sir Isaac Newton*
"LAWS OF MOTION"

"The First Law Of Motion. Oh my God, it's terrible."

"You scared?"

"Of course I'm scared. Who isn't? Aren't you?"

"No. Do you think everybody suffers from fear of flying?"

"No. But I think everybody suffers from fear of falling."

"Do you think this plane is likely to fall?"

"Planes are no more likely to fall than cars are likely to fly."

"Eminently sensible reply. So what's to be afraid of?"

"Cars don't fly because they *can't.*"

"Well, I've been flying for years. These planes are perfectly safe. There's nothing to be afraid of."

"Nothing to be afraid of? My God, didn't you hear her, that awful litany of 'unlikely events'? Sudden drop in air pressure! Water landing! Oh boy oh boy oh boy!?"

"Easy fella. There's nothing to worry about."

"I'm sitting in a thing that has four more exits than it has toilets and you're telling me there's nothing to worry about? What the hell is the matter with you? Didn't you catch the number she did on the exits? All that waving, pointing, my God, it was like looking at Swan Lake! Nobody has this many emergency exits unless there's a whole lot of other unlikely events she didn't bother mentioning!"

"Calm down. You're hysterical."

"Of course I'm hysterical! The knowledge that my seat cushion floats does not make me happy somehow! She says, in the unlikely event of a water landing I can use my seat cushion for floating, and suddenly I'm looking around for empty seats, figuring I'll grab a few extras and give myself an edge! I despise myself! I hate what I've become."

"Calm down."

"No way! I can just see the story in *The Inquirer:*

Man Survives Ninety Days on Lake Mead on Raft of Seat Cushions

Fashioned fishing tackle from headset he rented for three dollars, made fish hooks from staples holding baggage checks to ticket envelope, used shiny inside of plastic peanut wrapper as lure, lone survivor claims.

"I tell you, I hate myself! I'm filled with loathing!"

"Come on, fella, control yourself. Sit up straight."

"I can't. I'm in the recommended position for an emergency landing."

"But we haven't even taken off yet."

"Can't think of a better time to do it. Head down, arms locked under my legs. You know something? This position tells me that I will save my ass by absorbing the impact with my neck. I'd prefer it the other way around. I think I'll sit up."

"Now you're beginning to make sense."

"I'll just sit here and watch for the oxygen mask to automatically appear. I'll give it a sharp tug then place it over my nose and mouth and breath normally, but first I'll extinguish all smoking materials. I wonder if smoking materials are anything like cigarettes."

"That's what she meant. Cigarettes. You're being very silly."

"Normally? Breathe normally? You've got this stupid rubber thing on your face. You're wearing it like a mask. You are scared out of your mind. And she thinks I'm going to breathe normally? That girl is crazy!"

"Don't talk like that. She's just doing her job."

"You're right. Hell, I'm not really scared. You're a nice guy. And if worse comes to worse, you're welcome to ride on my raft."

"What are you up in the air about?"

"There are certain people who feel there is no sense in living unless something is blowing on them. The minute they get on a plane they turn on one of those blow-on-you things. But, they don't want it to hit them too directly, so they angle it so it hits the person next to them. And that is the reason the left side of my face is purple."

ALL ABOUT POOPING

poop \ püp \ n -ING/S often cap P&O&O&P [Perusal Of Other Passengers] the scanning of attitudes, behavior and actions of fellow passengers and crew members on a commercial airliner while in flight or while boarding or deplaning. "She favored the cabin with a deliberate poop, then stowed her carry-ons." S Berman unpblshd mnscrpt.

poop vt -ED/ING often cap P&O&O&P [from Perusal Of Other Passengers] to look around to see the expressions and actions of passengers and crew in the same plane as oneself in flight or while boarding or deplaning. "He sneaked aft to poop the smokers." S Berman unpblshd mnscrpt II. vi "Turbulence always set him to pooping." S Berman ibid.

WHY DO WE POOP?

We POOP to learn what's going on since so much of what happens with our flight seems to be none of our business. Airlines are loath to burden passengers with trivial bits of information. For example, they won't bother you with an explanation of why, twenty minutes after departure time, your plane is still standing at the gate with the door open, and then why, ten more minutes later, thirty people flock onto the plane.

Q. Why don't they just say what they're waiting for?

A. It's none of your business.

Airlines generously de-emphasize irksome details. If you're a smoker, for example, they don't dwell on where they are going to seat you. Why bother you with the fact that your seat barely manages to be on the inside of the plane? And it fully reclines, but in the wrong direction.

Q. Why don't they just tell smokers about their seats?

A. It's none of their damned business.

And if you're a non-smoker and request a non-smoking aisle seat, but you fail to be specific, the airline will not annoy you with petty details. They won't tell you you'll be in a DC-10 or an L-1011 and, yes you'll have an aisle seat, but you'll be in that center section where so many people hate to sit.

Q. Why don't they just say there are no more aisle seats near the window?

A. It's none of your damned business.

In the issuing of information the "company way" seems to be "tell them only what we have to tell them." The "cockpit way" seems to be "tell them much more than we have to tell them," but since most of us don't give a damn that Des Moines is on the left side of the plane, we don't listen.

The "Flight Attendant way" is the way we have all become so familiar with, familiar with, familiar with since we've heard it before, heard it before, heard it before. It's not the Flight Attendants' fault. They have to say these things though there are probably only three people on the plane who don't know there's no smoking in the lavatories, no smoking in the lavatories, no smoking in the lavatories, and they are little children.

The truth is Flight Attendants rarely say anything they don't have to say except "today" as in, "Care for a beverage today?" I can never understand that. I'm always tempted to answer, "No, but if I care for a beverage tomorrow is there someplace I can reach you?"

Anyway, since airlines feel so much is none of your damned business, you often find it necessary to POOP.

WHO POOPS?

Everybody POOPS. In a heavy POOPING situation you can be sure that whomever you are POOPING is POOPING you. Just as you are clever, subtle and sneaky about your POOPING, so are they.

Flight Attendants, being professional POOPERS, don't POOP like you POOP. They are trained to POOP only that which is POOPWORTHY. Before takeoff your lap is POOPWORTHY for the buckled seat belt check. In fact, just as your dentist is the only stranger who can get away with putting his fingers in your mouth, a Flight Attendant is the only one you'll allow to openly scrutinize your lap without your offering a protest or a proposition.

While Flight Attendants may be specialists in Pleasant and Efficient, they are not always specialists in public speaking. They have a disconcerting way of emphasizing wrong words in sentences, like, "The captain *has* turned off the 'No Smoking sign,'" as if someone has suggested the captain has *not* turned off the "No Smoking" sign.

Q. What is this chapter really trying to say?

A. It's none of your damned business. And since so much of what is going on with your flight remains undisclosed to you, all silences become suspect.

Q. What is the meaning of "inevitable"?

A. When you are in a three-seat row, all the tray tables are down and you're all having appetizers and drinks, the person in the window seat will have to go to the lavatory.

HEAVY POOPING SITUATIONS

WHEN YOU DON'T LISTEN TO THE COCKPIT ANNOUNCEMENT:

Because you have grown weary of hearing air speed and altitude and Des Moines is on the left side of the plane, you have learned to turn the cockpit announcements off. So you didn't hear, before takeoff, "We'll fly out over New York Harbor and circle back west on our way to Chicago." So you look out and think, "Oh my God, that's the Atlantic! I'm on a plane to Europe!" And you POOP to see if any others are on the wrong plane with you. And you discover you are the only one who got on the wrong plane! And then you realize the plane is turning.

WHEN THE FLIGHT ATTENDANT TURNS ON THE GALLEY FOOD WARMERS:

She knows this galley has seen better days. *She* knows it gives off a smell of something burning when it starts to heat up. But *you* don't know. *You* think, "Hey, is that smoke?" And you're not about to mention it to another passenger or ask the Flight Attendant about it because, if truth be told, you are more afraid of looking foolish than of going down in flames. So you POOP. You look for signs of concern in the other passengers and in the Flight Attendants. You look for others POOPING as well as you. You're not exactly panicking but you'd appreciate a bit of reassurance: "The smoke you smell is the normal smell of the landing gear locking into place."

WHEN WHICH WAY IS A SECRET:

Your plane lands at one of those small airports where you deplane outside of the terminal building. There's no airline agent there to direct you, and no signs indicating the correct way into the terminal. You stand aside and POOP. You do the POOP-AND-FOLLOW. Whichever way the others go you go. If they should walk to the edge of a cliff and leap down into a churning fjord you will not hesitate to go along.

WHEN THIS PLANE IS AN ICEBOX*:

You're absolutely freezing and nobody seems to notice. You POOP.

*See Chapter VIII, "YOU ARE THE ONLY ONE WHO'S FREEZING."

WHEN THIS PLANE IS A SAUNA:

Did you ever notice how Flight Attendants never feel cold or hot or hear strange noises in the engines or smell smoke? And if you happen to say it's hot, or it's cold, or that engine is making a strange noise, or I smell smoke, the Flight Attendant will smile at you as if you're not the first paranoid-schizophrenic she's ever dealt with. She'll say, you're hot? or you're cold? or you hear a noise? Or she'll say, you smell smoke? and she'll proceed to smell your entire vicinity as if you might be the cause of the untoward aroma, and all the other passengers will be POOPING in your direction and trying to figure out what you might have done to make the Flight Attendant do all that smelling. Next time you'll stick to POOPING and keep your mouth shut.

Q. When you're flying through a terrible storm, very bumpy, and lightning flashing all around, would that be one of your heavier POOP situations?

A. It's none of your damned business.

"What are you up in the air about?"

"They tell you about the exits and oxygen and tray tables and seatbacks and floating seat cushions. But they never tell you not to cross your legs. They never warn you about the person in front of you suddenly reclining his seat all the way back and locking your knees in the most excruciating jam you can imagine! You can't stay crossed, but you can't get uncrossed! It's a horrible, horrible thing!"

UNDERSTANDING YOUR FLIGHT ATTENDANT

or INTROS, FABGAB AND THE ALMIGHTY **"OH REALLY?"**

"...and my name is C_____, and I am your Inflight Services Coordinator."
P.A. address, DELTA AIRLINES

Inflight Services Coordinator is an example of FABGAB, the fabricated language of airlines. FABGAB serves a variety of functions, not the least of which is keeping passengers in awe. You hear you're on a plane with an Inflight Services Coordinator and you know right away these people know a lot more about airline stuff than you'll ever learn. You wouldn't dare open your mouth to them.

INTROS

Let us depart momentarily from FABGAB and get a handle on Flight Attendant introductions. You know how it goes:

"Your Flight Attendants in the main cabin are Nan, Marni and Lita, and in the forward cabin, Sheri and myself, Sue."

At this point let us take a short *Flight Attendant Introduction Effectivenss Test* (check the correct answer).

1. You're just dying to know the Flight Attendants' names.

    TRUE _____   FALSE _____

2. The last time you heard a Flight Attendant on the P.A. she was on a microphone
    _____ a. in the back of the plane.
    _____ b. in the middle of the plane.
    _____ c. in the front of the plane.
    _____ d. in a secret place as usual where it's impossible to see her, so you don't know who's talking or where she is and it drives you crazy when she introduces herself.

3. Where else might you be introduced to someone you can't see and be given four more names you are free to apply as you wish to any of those who happen to be in view? (check two answers)
    _____ a. At a party.
    _____ b. In a new place of employment.
    _____ c. In another airplane.
    _____ d. In the psychiatric ward of any county hospital.

SOME FABGAB SAMPLES

Sample #1. "MAIN CABIN/FORWARD CABIN"

Planes servicing two classes have a FORWARD CABIN and a MAIN CABIN.

Though you know that the words "FIRST" and "MAIN" are first cousins, you must struggle against the logic of this association since experience tells you FIRST CLASS is in the forward part of the plane.

Not only do FIRST CLASS passengers not get to sit in the MAIN CABIN, they don't even get to sit in the FIRST CLASS SECTION. This is because there *is* no FIRST CLASS SECTION, there is only the FORWARD CABIN.

The beauty of FABGAB: FIRST CLASS exists but is not recognized.

More beautiful, there is no SECOND CLASS. Thinking habits unwilling to die and antediluvian reasoning inform us that if there are two things and one of them is first the other must be second. The airlines know this is nonsense.

Just because a passenger isn't flying on a FIRST CLASS ticket is no reason to say the passenger is flying on a SECOND CLASS ticket. Such passengers are flying COACH.

Furthermore, COACH passengers do not sit in the COACH SECTION. There *is* no COACH SECTION. COACH passengers sit in the MAIN CABIN.

Sample #2. "COMPLIMENTARY"

There are only two ways for a beverage to be COMPLIMENTARY:
1. It has to be free of charge — "on the house."
2. It has to say, "You look marvelous!"
There is no recorded instance of a drink saying "You look marvelous!" Or anything else.

On a plane COMPLIMENTARY may not mean "free" but is FABGAB for "at no *extra* charge." (While for booze "there will be a charge" is FABGAB for "there will be an *extra* charge.") There is a neat way to check on the complimentariness of a COMPLIMENTARY drink. When the Flight Attendant offers you your COMPLIMENTARY coffee, tea, milk or soft drink, you say, "My doctor has me on a low-liquid diet. Could you please just give me the cash?"

Make a list of all the airlines that give you cash instead of the COMPLIMENTARY beverage. These airlines have proved they are ready to give you something for nothing.

1 . _____

Make a list of the airlines whose Flight Attendants laugh or run away from you when you ask for cash. Do not fly with these airlines. Be strong in your resolve. Let your motto be: FLY AMTRAK!

1 . _____
2 . _____
3 . _____
4 . _____

Sample #3. "LAVATORY"

When you're at home do you use the LAVATORY? No. You use the john or the toilet or, if you're putting on airs, the restroom. When you're at the theater or in a museum or at a ballpark or in an airport terminal, do you say, "Where's the LAVATORY?" No. You ask for the men's room or the ladies' room or the restroom.

LAVATORY used to be a real word, like "repast." It was big in England where today you might hear it only in its shortened form "LAV." In America, LAVATORY enjoyed a heyday in parochial schools in the '30's and '40's. Today LAVATORY is an airline word: FABGAB for toilet or restroom, etc.

The only ones who say LAVATORY today are Flight Attendants. But even they don't say LAVATORY all the time. When Flight Attendants are whispering together in the galley or in the back of the plane, they say toilet just like you and me.

THE ALMIGHTY "OH REALLY?"

The ALMIGHTY "OH REALLY?" is the immediate, ineluctable, reflexive response to anything a passenger might utter which smacks of something less than consummate satisfaction and a willing acceptance of whatever a flight has to offer.

"There's no magazine in the seat pocket in front of me."
"OH REALLY?"

41

"It's a bit chilly in here."*

"OH REALLY?"

What "OH REALLY?" does is create doubt. You can't hear it without second-guessing yourself.

"OH REALLY?" is another way of saying, "Are you absolutely certain of that?" "OH REALLY?" is another way of saying, "Come now, you must be joking." "OH REALLY?" is another way of saying,

*See Chapter VIII, "YOU ARE THE ONLY ONE WHO'S FREEZING."

"There are 212 other passengers on this plane, and I have spoken to each of them individually, and you are the only one on this flight, or on any of one thousand flights I have flown in my lifetime, to (e.g.) complain of a faulty call button. Do you want to stick with that complaint, or would you like a chance to think it over?" The ALMIGHTY "OH REALLY?" causes passengers to retreat.

"My tray table isn't level and my meal keeps sliding off."

"OH REALLY?"

"Ha ha, but I won't let it fall. Too hungry, ha ha."

"What are you up in the air about?"

"It drives me crazy! What makes them do it? I can't figure out why anybody would stop in an aisle, look directly at a person deeply engrossed in a novel and offer that person a magazine!"

Q. What is the origin of the famous phrase, "Your huddled masses yearning to breathe free..."?

A. Years ahead of her time, poet Emma Lazarus was describing flying Economy Class.

"THERE WILL BE A SLIGHT DELAY"

Q. At what point can you be reasonably certain of a delay in the departure of your flight?

A. When you make your reservation.

I. THE MEANING OF SLIGHT DELAY

The expression SLIGHT DELAY implies there are delays which are not slight. But when have you heard an airline say there will be a long delay? Long delays are not acknowledged. When an airline SLIGHT DELAY ceases being slight the delay becomes a CHANGED-TO or a NOW-SCHEDULED-TO-DEPART-AT.

In order to make the SLIGHT DELAY workable and acceptable, the airlines had to make two determinations:

1. That the length of a SLIGHT DELAY is ten minutes.

2. That the airlines alone know the meaning of "ten minutes."

Since airlines regard ten minutes as hardly noticeable, passengers are rarely informed of this barely measurable delay unless a passenger makes an inquiry. Inquiries early in a SLIGHT DELAY are rarely made, however, since most of us prefer to be GLIPS (Good Little Passengers). When a passenger *does* inquire, the answer will be, "We'll be boarding in about ten minutes."

"Ten minutes," is not responsive since it ignores the reason for the passenger inquiry to begin with. You don't ask about a delay unless you've already been waiting awhile; let's say ten minutes. So, this ten minutes plus the next ten minutes comes to at least a twenty-minute delay. Now SLIGHT DELAY takes on a quality of incipient foreverness.

II. EGADS — ENIGMATIC GATE AREA DELAY SITUATION

The major characteristic of an EGADS is silence. Airlines do not volunteer delay talk. They wait to be asked. When you do go up to an airline person and say, "We were supposed to take off twenty minutes ago and we haven't boarded yet," the airline person will offer with almost amused assurance, "We'll be boarding in about ten minutes."

It is important to understand that DELAYS ARE CALCULATED IN INCREMENTS OF TEN MINUTES. In an EGADS there is no such thing as a 30-minute delay, but only a 10-minute delay 3 times.

Q. What happens if you want to complain about a half-hour delay?

A. You can only complain about one ten-minute delay at a time.

III. PAT PHRASES

When the airline uses up its self-imposed quota of ten-minute assurances it moves to other effective pacifiers like, "We'll be boarding any time now." This is *always* accompanied by some physicalization on the part of the airline person.

1. An abrupt move away as if in a great hurry to do something of enormous importance.

2. An immediate duck down behind the check-in counter as if something terribly urgent has just occurred down there.

IV. $A = fr^2$
or AGGRAVATION EQUALS FANTASY TIMES REALITY SQUARED

There are two kinds of delay times: PASSENGER REALITY TIME and AIRLINE FANTASY TIME. AFT is what the airline tells you. PRT is what the delay might actually come to.

ANTICIPATED DEPARTURE DELAY
COMPARISON TABLE

AFT	PRT
10 min	35 min
20 min	1.4 hr
30 min	2-3 hr
1 hr	canceled

CAUTION: You never know when an airline will decide to use PRT. Even veteran passengers have fallen into the trap of thinking the airline will never let a plane depart when they say it will. They leave the gate area only to come back and discover they've missed the plane.

Q. Do planes scheduled to leave ten minutes late ever actually leave ten minutes late?

A. Try as they do for perfection, airlines sometimes let a delay slip through their fingers and a plane will leave only ten minutes late as the airline said.

V. SLIGHT DELAY — CAUSES

MECHANICAL: Something is not working or a red light warns of unsafe conditions. Mechanicals are never discovered until all the passengers are checked in and boarded or waiting to board, and all competing flights going to the same destination are full or have taken off.

EQUIPMENT: Late arrival of equipment. You don't fly in a plane, you fly in equipment. "Fog had the equipment stuck in Chicago for two hours. It ought to be here in about ten minutes."

TRAFFIC: "They were on hold up there for twenty minutes. We'll be boarding momentarily."

SECRET: This is the most common cause of delay. It unfailingly takes place in the gate area. It simply gets later and later and nobody seems to notice but you. The airline says absolutely nothing.

VI. SECRET DELAY OR CREELAY (CREEPING DELAY) AT WORK

You arrive at the airport a half-hour before flight time as directed. You check the FLYBY AIRWAYS screen: your flight, 86, will depart at 1:22P from Gate 78. On time. Fine.

You hurry to the gate and check in with the "AGENT-AT-THE-GATE" (you never know how to refer to these people). You get your seat selection and then sit down in the gate area and read your book.

 TIME PASSES

Your watch says 1:07P. It's fifteen minutes prior to flight time; time to board the plane. The sign on the wall says Flight 86 is still scheduled to depart at 1:22P. You POOP the area. It is mobbed. Nobody seems the least bit concerned. The AIRLINE PERSONS are being pleasant and efficient.

 TIME PASSES

1:17P. Nothing is happening. The AIRLINE PERSONS are smiling and busy as if everything's going just fine. The departure sign still says 1:22P. You know that even if they started boarding this very second the plane could not possibly depart at 1:22P. You POOP the area. You realize you are the only one who's wondering about it.

TIME PASSES

1:20P. Two minutes to takeoff. No way. You say to a man seated near you, "Looks like we're in for a bit of a delay here." He says, "Yep," and goes back to his newspaper. You're in the TWILIGHT ZONE! You think to yourself, "Sure. It's okay for this guy to be indifferent. He doesn't have to make a connection in Dallas. He doesn't have to attend the most important meeting of his entire life!"

 TIME PASSES

1:32P! The sign still says 1:22P! There is no way on earth this plane can depart at 1:22P, unless they're talking about *tomorrow*! WHY DON'T THEY SAY SOMETHING? WHY DON'T THEY AT LEAST SAY THEY KNOW ABOUT THE DELAY? WHY ARE THEY MAKING ME SUFFER LIKE THIS?

You saunter over to the check-in counter and look at the pleasant AIRLINE PERSONS. One is doing magic with someone's ticket. The other is telling someone this is not the flight for Nepal. Now, one looks up at you, smiles and walks away. You address the other.

"Is there going to be some kind of delay?"

"No. We'll be leaving on time."

"How can we do that? I have 1:33, and we're supposed to leave at 1:22."

"We'll be boarding momentarily."

Q. How do you feel about this AIRLINE PERSON?

A. You feel like putting on hunting boots and jumping on this AIRLINE PERSON'S insteps.

VII. THE CREELAY ENDS

The CREELAY ends with, "Ladies and gentlemen, FLYBY AIRWAYS' FLIGHT 86 for Dallas is now boarding at Gate 78. Please have your boarding passes available for collection by the agent at the gate. We apologize for the delay."

THEY KNEW IT! THEY KNEW IT ALL THE TIME! AND THEY APOLOGIZE! AND THEY WILL *CONTINUE* TO APOLOGIZE ALL THE WAY THROUGH THE FLIGHT! FOREVER! THEY *HAVE* APOLOGIZED, AND THEY *WILL*:

APOLOGIZE!

". . .exit doors on either side of four windows directly over your carry-on baggage under the mask over your attendants now demonstrating with infants and small uniformed crew member equipped with floatable unlikely water belt for easy fastening low and tight across your tray tables and ONCE AGAIN WE'D LIKE TO APOLOGIZE FOR THE DELAY AND THANK YOU FOR YOUR PATIENCE AND HOPE YOU HAVE A PLEASANT FLIGHT THANK YOU."

and

APOLOGIZE!

". . .airborne we invite you to relax your luncheon and enjoy our three dollars in the main Flight Attendant coming through the panel over your shoulder or in audio selections to the complimentary purchase AGAIN WE'D LIKE TO APOLOGIZE FOR THE DELAY AND THANK YOU FOR YOUR PATIENCE AND HOPE YOU HAVE A PLEASANT FLIGHT THANK YOU."

and

APOLOGIZE!

". . .altitude of thirty six thousand miles per Palm Springs crossing Arizona diagonally over the western tip of seat belts when you're LIKE TO APOLOGIZE FOR THE DELAY AND THANK YOU FOR YOUR PATIENCE AND HOPE YOU HAVE A PLEASANT FLIGHT THANK YOU."

and

APOLOGIZE!

". . . Dallas Fort Worth seat belts coming to a complete stop at the choosing FLYBY AIRWAYS for the pleasure of serving you again in the APOLOGIZE FOR THE DELAY AND THANK YOU FOR YOUR PATIENCE AND HOPE YOU HAD A PLEASANT FLIGHT THANK YOU."

Q. What is the silliest, most annoying, most impossible to obey sign that can light up in a plane?

A. "RETURN TO YOUR SEAT." The sign is activated by raising the toilet lid.

WHOSE VOICE IS THAT AND WHY IS IT SAYING THESE THINGS?

Years ago, when a male voice got on the P.A., you knew it was the CAPTAIN. First of all, in those days the Captain's was the only male voice that ever got on the P.A. Secondly, he'd introduce himself. "'Uh — good morning — uh — this is — uh — your — uh — pilot — uh — Captain Holbrook." Right then and there you knew exactly who was talking to you.

Today it's different. Today that male voice on the P.A. could belong to just about anybody — the SECOND OFFICER, the THIRD OFFICER or a MALE FLIGHT ATTENDANT. And it has become very rare for the speaker to introduce himself, even if he's the CAPTAIN. You just never hear, "Hi there, folks, I'm your MALE FLIGHT ATTENDANT," or, "Hi there, this is your COPILOT speaking," or, "Hi there, I am a deranged passenger trying to get into show business."

Q. Why is the cockpit crew so insistent on anonymity?

A. In a worldwide survey over a period of forty years, the results indicated that the people most likely to let you hear their voices but not identify themselves are 1. FLIGHT ENGINEERS and COPILOTS, and 2. OBSCENE PHONE-CALLERS.

Q. Is this suggestive of any correlative conclusions?

A. On the contrary. In another survey among airline passengers worldwide, the conclusions were that 96% of those who have listened to cockpit announcements would prefer obscene phone calls.

I. DISTINGUISHING COCKPIT P.A. FROM FLIGHT ATTENDANT P.A.

It used to be a snap, but with the introduction of the Male Flight Attendant most passengers, hearing a male voice on the P.A., could not tell, for at least the first part of the announcement, whether they were listening to a COCKPIT AN-NOUNCEMENT or a FLIGHT ATTENDANT ANNOUNCEMENT.

All COCKPIT ANNOUNCEMENTS have distinguishing characteristics:

If the P.A. comes when you are peacefully asleep IT IS A COCKPIT ANNOUNCEMENT.

Though not always the case, one sure-fire give-away is the audible-inaudible P.A. If the announcement has too low a volume for you to make out what is being said, but it is loud enough to wake you from sleep and cause you to sit there wondering what the hell happened to your hearing, IT IS A COCKPIT ANNOUNCEMENT.

Context is purely the most important indicator of P.A. type. There is no mistaking certain references and sounds. If the P.A. contains the words "air," "about," "weather," "tail wind," "left side," "right side," and the very frequent use of "uh," IT IS A COCKPIT ANNOUNCEMENT.

Listen also for the *vital non sequitur*. If the P.A. contains something like, "Uh, we are, uh, just passing over the, uh, extreme western tip of, uh, the Oklahoma Panhandle," IT IS A COCKPIT ANNOUNCEMENT. It is called "vital" because of the off chance that knowing the plane is passing over the extreme western tip of the Oklahoma Panhandle might be important to *somebody*.

Q. Isn't this very considerate of the COCKPIT PEOPLE?

A. It warms the heart. Two or three hundred people have their work stopped, their conversations interrupted, their nap stopped, just so some seaweed-brain can press his forehead to a window and look thirty-five thousand feet down to see the extreme western tip of the Oklahoma Panhandle. It makes one weep.

COCKPIT ANNOUNCEMENT VALUE AND COMPREHENSION TEST

1. "Uh, we are, uh, flying at an altitude of, uh, thirty-four thousand feet." We are told this so we will know:
    a.__ It would be silly to consider getting out of the plane at this time.
    b.__ We don't have to worry about trees and high tension wires.
    c.__ If we're ever at a cocktail party and the conversation turns to altitude, we can offer a salient comment or two on what it's like in the thirty thousands.

2. "Over, uh, Albuquerque, then, uh, across the, uh, extreme western tip of the, uh, Oklahoma Panhandle, then, uh, crossing the, uh, the Missouri River, in the, uh, vicinity of, uh, Kansas City." We are told this so we will know:
    a.__ We are going in the right direction so we don't have to worry that we got on the wrong plane.
    b.__ New Mexico, Oklahoma, Kansas and the Missouri River are exactly where they were last month.

c.__ We can relax because those guys up front sure as hell know the way Chicago.

3. "Our air speed is, uh, six hundred miles per hour." We are told this so we will know:
a.__ We're going fast enough to stay up.
b.__ We are witnessing Einstein's Theory Of Relativity. No matter how fast we travel we will still arrive late.
c.__ If we're ever at a cocktail party and the conversation turns to speed, we can offer a salient comment or two on what it's like in the six hundreds.

4. "That's, uh, Pike's Peak on our, uh, left." We are told this so we will know:
a.__ Once again we're sitting on the wrong side of the plane.
b.__ The movie projector must be on the fritz. Since airlines began showing movies it is very rare to hear about Pike's Peak. A whole new generation has grown up thinking Pike's Peak is a reference to the way a fish looks at a bait.
c.__ Those of us who can see it can determine once and for all that seeing Pike's Peak from a passenger jet is possibly the most boring experience in the world.

Q. Does this chapter intend to say COCKPIT ANNOUNCEMENTS are unnecessary?

A. This chapter acknowledges COCKPIT AN-NOUNCEMENTS are necessary. It also acknowledges that sometimes root-canal is necessary.

"What are you up in the air about?"

"The woman behind me went to the lavatory every ten minutes. Each time she went she used my seatback to pull herself up. When she came back she used my seatback to lower herself down. My seatback would go back a good four inches and then she'd let go, snapping it like a catapult with my head as the missile. Oh, what a headache I've got."

THE
TOY MEALS

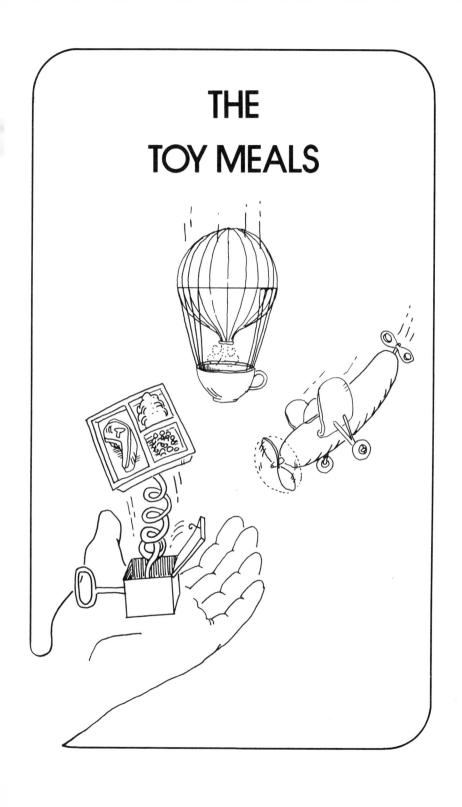

Most airlines haven't yet gotten around to serving catsup. This is because no airline serves French fries. It's a shame.

French fries would be incompatible with the airline practice of serving TOY MEALS. Airlines, in case you haven't noticed, serve miniaturized meals, but in such a way as to make it look like you're getting too much to eat. They give you little toy knives, little toy forks, little toy dishes, little toy vegetables, little toy steaks covered with little toy epoxy gravy. It's cute.

A life-size French fry is a long thing. Whittling it down to toy size would be costly and wasteful. But serving a real French fry might invite questions about the portions of other items on the same plate. A passenger might reason that, since there is no such thing as giant French fries, that other thing on the plate must be a miniature filet mignon.

Q. Would an airline have the gall to serve a toy filet mignon?

A. If they have the gall to serve a packet of eleven peanuts to a person having a Scotch on the rocks they're not likely to be bashful about serving a toy filet mignon.

Q. Airline filet mignons are nevertheless tasty, aren't they?

A. People who like their filet mignons boiled rave about them.

THE TECHNIQUES OF MINIATURIZING:

It's all in the toy plates. Look at your next airline meal. See how the food slops over the edge of the plate. One touch of a fork will send food sliding off the plate. You won't think, "This plate is too small." You'll think, "There's too much food here."

Remember, you are not in the real world up there. Forget the meal for a moment. Look around you. Look at the lavatory. Is that a real lavatory? No, it is a toy lavatory. Look at the window near your seat. It is a toy window. Your reading light is a toy light and it has a toy switch. Look at your pillow. Just big enough for your dolly, isn't it? Cover yourself with your blanket. It's a toy blanket. Listen! You and the Flight Attendant are speaking in toy sentences!

THE TOY GARNISHES:

Q. Where might you find a whole tomato, a whole pitted black olive and a whole sweet gherkin all stuck on one ordinary toothpick?

A. On an airline light lunch plate, either pinning the sandwich or lying next to it.

Q. How is it possible to put so much on one toothpick?

A. Toys. What you have is a toy tomato, a toy black olive. A gherkin is a toy pickle to begin with. But there are such things as midget gherkins as well; or *toy* toy pickles. Airlines find *small* midget gherkins; *toy* toy toy pickles! There is talk that toothpick garnishes are put together by retired watchmakers.

Most of us truly cherish garnishes; the crisp, moist, tangy taste delights that accompany our sandwich. We hate to be out of garnish before we are out of sandwich. We pace ourselves: bite of sandwich, nibble of gherkin, bite of sandwich, nibble of olive.

Airlines are woefully indifferent to the concept of coordinated sandwich/garnish eating. Let us look at a comparison of sandwich life to garnish life airline style.

SANDWICH LIFE:
(The rare life-size sandwich)
12 good bites for normal eaters.
14 for most women, well-bred men and sissies.

GARNISH LIFE:

GHERKIN: 2 small nibbles at best.
TOMATO: Plop whole in mouth. Attempting to bite can result in squirting mess. Count 1 food nibble.
OLIVE: 1.5 tiny nibbles.

      12.0 Sandwich Bites
    - 4.5 Garnish Nibbles
    ─────
       7.5 Unaccompanied Sandwich Bites

HOW MUCH IS NOT ENOUGH?

One day some people (not necessarily airline people) decided to package condiments in such a way as to make the contents not enough. Packaging materials were selected. Exact amounts of not enough were determined and standardized. Places to "Tear Here" were invented and refined.

Today we in the free world enjoy the convenient and ubiquitous little packets of not enough mustard, not enough mayonnaise, not enough catsup.

Marvelous little not enough salt and pepper shakers came into common use, particularly on airlines. These are the little toy corduroy paper shakers you open by breaking their back. This makes the cleverly channeled belly burst and spew salt all over the place. This is why you so often see passengers taking a bite of meat and then licking their lap.

Serving not enough salad dressing varies with the airlines.* Sometimes it's the size of the little plastic cup, sometimes it's just the amount in the cup. Some airlines have come up with the most ingenious solution of all — lousy salad dressing. They give it a

---

*In First Class, salad dressing is ladled on by the Flight Attendant. In the overall breakdown this single service might run you about $42.57.

catchy name: "Vinaigrette Pago Pago." They figure you'll hate it but you'll blame Pago Pago, not the airline. And you'll find that not enough is actually too much.

COPING WITH YOUR TOY MEAL TRAY:

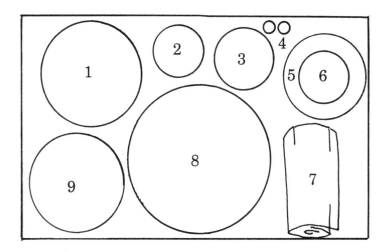

First of all, you must identify the items on the tray, then you must understand them.

1. SALAD PLATE: Most times the salad is already on the plate when you get it. It is easy to recognize. Look for two yellowish tomato quarters and one thick lump of unseparated

lettuce leaves. There is no way to mix the dressing into the salad without half the salad falling off the plate. It makes you feel as if you have too much.

2.   SALAD DRESSING: "Creme d'Alsace Lorraine." It will taste suspiciously like the "Creme de Napoli à la Pope Leo" you had on the flight out. The little dressing cup will be on the tray rather than on the salad plate since breathing room is intolerable.

3.   WINE GLASS: An effective tray-crammer, especially if you don't drink wine. If you order a soft drink or a beer they will bring you a can and another glass and run off without taking the wine glass. You will spend most of your mealtime looking for a place to put the can and new glass.

4.   SALT AND PEPPER: These are the paper jobs you have to break open, losing considerable salt or pepper and being forced to lick your lap. Sometimes you get little plastic cylinders with sticky paper over the holes so the salt won't fall out. You peel off the sticky paper and find three little holes, and inside, three little grains of salt.

5.&6. CUP AND SAUCER: When flying you need to consume liquids like you need a nosebleed.* A good rule is DON'T DRINK AND FLY.

7. THE NAPKIN AND SILVER PUZZLE: Inside the cunningly folded napkin are your knife, fork and spoon. The object is to get these cleverly secreted items out of the napkin without one or more of them dropping out onto the floor. You, trapped by your tray table, will not be able to retrieve fallen items. You will have to ask for replacements, which is the same as saying, "I am an ass who can't unfold a napkin without losing my fork." Sometimes the silver comes in a clear plastic sleeve which can be opened only with a Samurai sword.

8. BREAD AND BUTTER PLATE: Dinner roll and butter are life-size. Sometimes your dessert cake comes on the same plate. The cake, too, is life-size, unfortunately.

*See Chapter IX, "ON THE DIFFERENCE BETWEEN VACANT AND OCCUPIED."

THE MENU
CALLING A SPADE A SHOVEL

"It has been our pleasure to prepare this repast for your enjoyment."
Menu statement, Executive Chef, United Airlines

Just for the hell of it, take a moment of silence and ask yourself, "How many times have I said, written or thought the word 'repast' in my entire life to this day?" If you are 25 or under it is all right to look the word up in your dictionary before taking your moment of silence. If you are between 25 and 54 and you have used *repast* six or more times in your life, you probably are suffering from a serious dysfunction of every gland in your whole body. If you are 54 and over and you've used *repast* 12 or more times, you have not been invited to a party in close to 32 years.

*"Shrimps, Scallops, Cod and Crabmeat in a Sauce of
Fish Broth, Herbs and Spices. Presented on a bed of
Mazzurelle Pasta Shells and served with Broccoli
Florets."*
Menu Offering, Ambassador Class, TWA

"Hey, Vinnie? Who's Mazzurelle?"

"Never heard of him."

"He's on the menu. Mazzurelle pasta shells. Is he
the guy who invented them or something?"

*"I wouldn't know. Maybe he's not a person. Maybe
he's a kind of flour, like semolina. You sure you read
it right? You sure it doesn't say mozzarella?"*

"Hand to God. Mazzurelle. Capital M. Who puts
a capital M on mozzarella except if it begins a
sentence?"

*"Maybe it's a brand name. Or the chef's name like
in fancy restaurants. Why don't you just forget it?"*

"I can't forget it. I want to be sure Mazzurelle isn't Italian for green. I hate green pasta. It makes me sick."

"It doesn't mean green. That I know."

"Why do they do it, Vinnie? Why do they keep putting words in the menu nobody can understand? On the flight out, yesterday, I had *savoyarde* potatoes. And today I can't even remember what they looked like or tasted like. I've got total amnesia about savoyarde potatoes."

"Me too. I fly First Class a lot and savoyarde potatoes are a heavy number up there. But I still can't picture them. Baked, mashed, even au gratin, I feel a sense of belonging with that. But I never walked into the house and said, "Hey, Angela, I'm just dying for a big scoop of savoyarde potatoes."

"Tomato clamart. How does that grab you?"

"It drives me nuts. I saw it once on a First Class menu. I asked the Flight Attendant what it was. She was totally stumped. She asked the Flight Engineer and, believe it or not, even he didn't know. So I just figured the hell with it and ordered a different repast."

"That's another one. I never tasted repast."

"Forget it. Anyway, I went crazy trying to find out about tomato clamart. I looked in Julia Child, Larousse Gastronomique, Craig Claiborne, Webster's International. Nothing."

"Vinnie, there's a good chance we'll go to our graves never knowing the truth about tomato clamart and Mazzurelle."

"Twenty years from now I'm going to wake up in the middle of the night and say, 'Mazzurelle? Who the hell, what the hell, is Mazzurelle?'"

Q. **What is the best way to avoid having your baggage lost when traveling by air?**

A. **Go by bus.**

"What are you up in the air about?"

"I'm an airborne contradiction. I fly First Class but I drink beer. It's very hard for them to understand this up front. Up front you're supposed to prefer wine. Before we take off they offer me champagne. I say I'd rather have a beer. They serve my meal and say, 'Red wine or white wine?' I say beer. They don't bother taking the wine glass off my tray because they know I can't possibly mean what I'm saying. They ask what kind of beer I'd like. I ask what kind they've got. They go away and come back. They say I can have my choice of beer — frozen beer or warm beer. I say give me a coke. They bring me a coke. Later on they come back and say, 'Care for more wine?' "

YOU ARE THE ONLY ONE WHO'S FREEZING

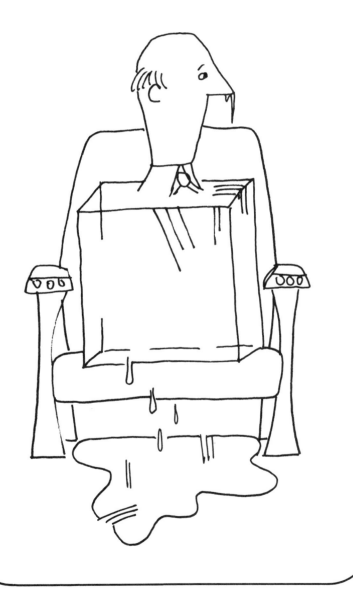

The nobody-else-is-cold-but-you phenomenon generally occurs on shorter, single-class flights. Somewhere between the time the seatbelt/no smoking signs go off and the plane reaches altitude, the captain flips a switch which converts an everyday passenger plane into a refrigerator car. Why is this? Your guess is as good as anybody else's.

- It's too warm in the cockpit?
- It's a service to the passengers; the airline is doing its part to keep the passengers from spoiling?

When you are feeling chilly on a plane you are in a definite POOP situation. You want company in this. You want support. You want to know that other passengers are also feeling chilly. You certainly don't want to be the only one on the plane to question this airline's temperature selection and the crew's ability to carry it off. But your initial POOP (as always) will yield little support. Nobody will seem the least bit cold. The men will be in shirtsleeves, the women in light cotton prints, all cozily going about the business of being GLIPS (Good Little Passengers). You will hate yourself for your watery blood!

Q. Why can't you just say to a Flight Attendant, "It's freezing on this plane"?

A. Because the Flight Attendant will zonk you with an ALMIGHTY "OH REALLY?"* She will say, "Oh really?" as if this is the last thing in her whole life she ever expected to hear, and you are the only one on the plane who would say such a thing. You will immediately back down: "Maybe it's just my imagination. I'm anemic, you know."

*See Chapter III, "UNDERSTANDING YOUR FLIGHT ATTENDANT."

It gets worse. Flight Attendants don't stop with the "OH REALLY?" She (or he) will then reach in and feel your overhead vents. Then she'll tighten them even though they're not blowing. She will ignore you even as you meekly protest, "They're not blowing."

Q. Why does the Flight Attendant feel your overhead air vents and tighten them even if they're not blowing?

A. 1. This ritualized pantomime is performed to let you know there is no possible way for you to be freezing on this plane unless you yourself did something to make it cold.

2. Flight Attendants are convinced you wouldn't know if an overhead air vent was blowing on your head and making you cold.*

3. Flight Attendants are also convinced that, even if you did know an air vent was blowing on your head, you wouldn't know enough to reach up and turn it off, if in fact you knew *how* to reach up and turn it off.

---

*OVERHEAD AIR VENT seems insufficiently descriptive. A better term might be "blow-on-you-thing."

KEEP ON POOPING! As you continue your Perusal Of Other Passengers you will begin to see supportive activity: shivering, rubbing of upper arms, people putting on sweaters or reaching for blankets. SEIZE THE MOMENT! Say, "Wow! It's freezing in here!" When the Flight Attendant says, "Oh really?" shout, "You betcha! Look around!"

Q. Will something now be done about the cold?

A. Yes. They will turn on the heat. It will get unbearably hot in the plane. You will have to turn on the blow-on-you-thing for the rest of the flight.

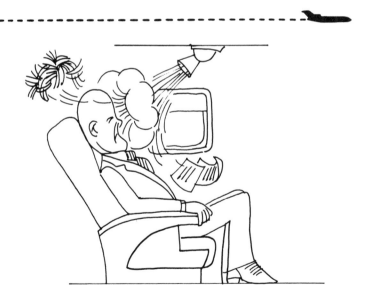

Q. What is the "could-I-ask-just-one-question-please" situation?

A. You're in a hurry to catch a plane yet you need to ask a question, but all the agents are busy. So you ignore the lines of people, charge the counter, interrupt a busy agent and say, "Could I ask just one question, please?"

Q. Is there an alternative for those who lack the nerve to do this?

A. Yes. You simply go to the end of the line in the appropriately roped maze. When you finally reach the agent you may ask your question: "Is it all right for me to just go ahead and check in at the gate, or do I have to wait in this line?"

ON THE DIFFERENCE BETWEEN VACANT AND OCCUPIED

Q. Other than the sun'll come up tomorrow, what can any of us really be sure of?

A. After the movie there will be a run on the lavatories.

Q. What if it's a flight without a movie?

A. Don't get your hopes up. You'll wait anyway.

There are two signs which light up over the lavatories:
VACANT — the only word that matters
OCCUPIED — the lavatory's natural state

VACANT illuminated means:
1. The lavatory is not in use and you may go in.
2. The lavatory *is* in use but the person inside forgot to lock the door.

OCCUPIED illuminated means:
1. That woman with the makeup case in one hand and the child in the other has just beat you to it.
2. This room is closed to the public because of equipment problems, or someone has died in here and you are the only one who cares.

NUMBERS MOST WONDERFUL AND WORRISOME:

A full 747 Coach Section might contain 339 persons.

A full DC-10 Coach Section might contain 260 persons.

A full 727 Coach Section might contain 120 persons.

———————————————————

A 747 Coach Section has 8 lavatories:
$339 \div 8 = 42.375$ ppl*

A DC-10 Coach Section has 6 lavatories:
$260 \div 6 = 43.33$ ppl.

A 727 Coach Section has 2 lavatories:
$120 \div 2 = 60$ (SIXTY!) ppl.

Q. What is the important message conveyed by these figures?

A. Thank God they don't show movies on 727's!

*ppl — persons per lavatory

NUMBERS DON'T LIE:

However slim the chances may be, there remains the distinct possibility that someday, when you're on a 727, you might find yourself last in a line of 59 persons waiting to get into the lavatory. It will be a terrible thing.

Q. Isn't 59 a rather fanciful figure, and its chances of actually occurring just about nil?

A. It doesn't matter, since for reasons not quite understood, when you want to use the lavatory on a flying plane, waiting for 4 people feels exactly the same as waiting for 59 people.

Q. What are the odds of your getting into the lavatory first?

A. According to actual surveys taken over a ten-year period among tourists, business people and students, the conclusions are that the odds in favor of your getting into an airline lavatory first are one-tenth of one percent less than the odds in favor of your being struck by lightening in Mammoth Cave.

CONCLUSION: DRINKING AND FLYING DON'T MIX.

"What are you up in the air about?"

"Five full hours that kid kept kicking the back of my seat! Five full hours! Through lunch! Through the movie! Kicking, kicking!"

Q. What happens to baggage that goes on first?

A. It comes off last.

GOING INTO AN AIRPORT YOU'RE NOT TOO FAMILIAR WITH AND WANTING TO PARK SOMEWHERE IN THE VICINITY OF THE TERMINAL SO YOU CAN MEET SOMEBODY, FOR GOD'S SAKE!

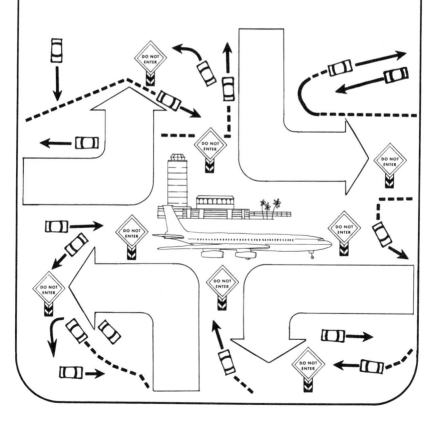

There it is! Just like they told you at the motel.

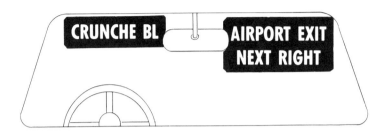

So you make a right off the freeway and...

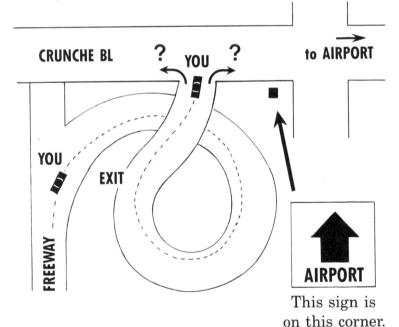

This sign is
on this corner.

...voila! You are LOST!

FINALLY!

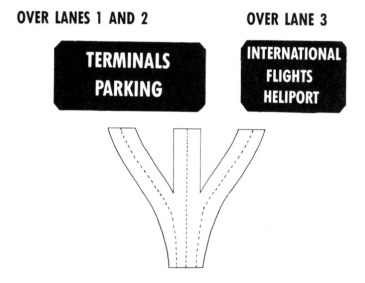

METROPOLITAN INTERNATIONAL AIRPORT — WELCOME

A beautiful, wonderful sign telling you you're in the right place! You drive in, under the sign which spans three driving lanes. You move on to:

OVER LANES 1 AND 2

TERMINALS PARKING

OVER LANE 3

INTERNATIONAL FLIGHTS HELIPORT

For the moment lane 3 is no great concern, but 1 and 2 present a small worry: you are headed in the right direction for TERMINALS and PARKING, but does this sign mean both are in the same place? Or should you stay in lane 1 for TERMINALS and 2 for PARKING? If there's a traffic buildup things could get sticky if you happen to be in the wrong lane. What's it say up ahead?

Wait a minute! What did they do with PARKING? You are looking for PARKING! You have to meet HARLEY FARLEY at the gate, at FLYBY AIRWAYS! Yes, you see the ARRIVALS sign, and HARLEY *is* arriving, but first you have to park — park near FLYBY AIRWAYS so you can go to the gate and meet him. What did they do with PARKING?

Did you miss it? Oh my God, could you have missed the PARKING sign? It's 3:55 and his plane lands at 4:10. He's your boss! Your *boss*! Look! More signs!

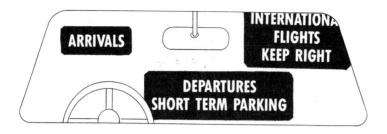

SHORT-TERM PARKING? Is that different from plain PARKING? Is there LONG-TERM PARKING? Was there a sign for LONG-TERM PARKING? It doesn't matter. You'd better move over into lane 2 just in case. Wait a minute! That sign said DEPARTURES! DEPARTURES and SHORT-TERM PARKING! You don't want DEPARTURES! You want ARRIVALS! You want PARKING near ARRIVALS — near FLYBY AIRWAYS ARRIVALS.

Okay. Look for traffic. Now move over to lane 2. Great. Look! More signs up ahead. They'll explain everything. Please, God.

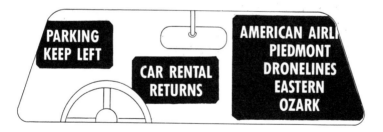

OH BOY! GET BACK INTO LANE 1! FAST! Whatever happened to SHORT-TERM PARKING?

Probably not what you wanted anyway. That sign with AMERICAN on it, it had a whole list of other airlines. You went by a bit fast. You were looking for PARKING. For ARRIVALS. Oh boy! Was FLYBY AIRWAYS on that sign? Long list. Did you miss FLYBY?

How did it happen!? How did you get yourself trapped in CAR RENTAL RETURNS? You were looking for plain PARKING! Nothing else! MOVE OVER! MOVE TO THE RIGHT OR DIE TRYING!

What did those other two signs say? Was FLYBY AIRWAYS on that long list? And RETURN TO AIRPORT? Why? Did you leave it? When did you leave the damned airport? PARKING! PLEASE, GOD! You'll take any kind of PARKING! LONG-TERM, SHORT-TERM, MEDIUM! Anything!

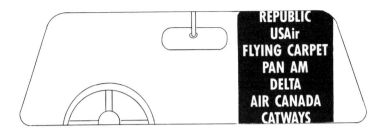

That's it? Nothing for lanes 1 and 2? Was it something you said? *PARKING! FLYBY!* Where are they? Why are they doing this to you? It's like one of those TV weather reports where you're sitting in maybe Gary, Indiana dying to find out if it's going to rain on your picnic tomorrow, and the weather person keeps telling you what to expect in Boston! A sign! A sign! Please, just one good sign!

Metered? What's metered? When did that happen? What happened to good old SHORT-TERM just plain PARKING? Lane 2 says PARKING. Swell.

You'll take it. Freeways, hotels, it doesn't matter, you'll take it. The only thing left is to find FLYBY AIRWAYS. If you could just see one sign saying FLYBY AIRWAYS, you'll have it made.

What's that sign just up ahead? That ought to be it.

Q. Do airlines take your contact phone number so they can call you in the event of a flight cancellation or delay?

A. Of course not. It is common knowledge that 98% of all cancellations and prolonged delays arise only during that period when passengers are en route to the airport.

Q. Why do airlines frequently get all the passengers boarded before announcing there's going to be a delay?

A. Notice that the engines are idling. It is all a special service designed to relieve passengers of their delay anxieties by shifting their concern to the question of whether or not they will survive the fumes.

OH THE BAGGAGE COMES OUT HERE AN' YOUR BAG GOES ROUN' AN' ROUN' WOH-OH-OH-OH-OH-OH AN' IT GOES OUT THERE

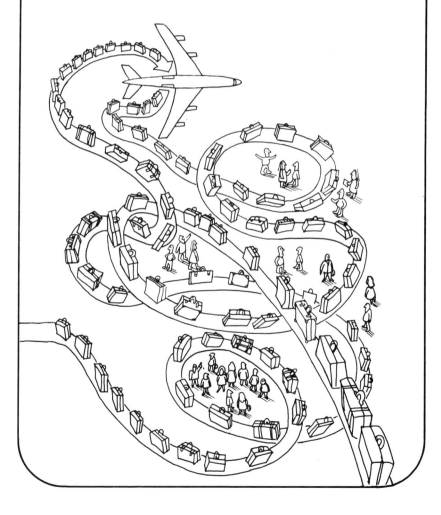

Q. Where might you find atheists at prayer?

A. In an airport baggage claim area.

Q. Are they afraid they will lose their baggage?

A. They are afraid they will lose their minds.

Airlines have two favorite kinds of conveyors to deliver your baggage to you at the end of a flight. Both require the passenger to have speed, patience, strength and a will to succeed. Also helpful would be a Zen Buddhist approach to certain questions, like: "How come the sign over this conveyor says 'Flight 118' while the tags on the bags on this conveyor say 'Flight 379' and I was told to come to this conveyor for my baggage from Flight 465?"

On one type of conveyor the baggage comes out through a slitted leather curtain over a hole in the wall. It moves around on a long conveyor belt until it disappears through another hole in the wall. WOH-OH-OH-OH-OH-OH AN' IT GOES OUT THERE.

The other favorite is the CAROUSEL. The baggage comes down a chute, then travels continuously in an ellipsoidal route chillingly suggestive of infinity. AN' YOUR BAG GOES ROUN' AND ROUN'.

For ease and clarity we'll call both types CAROUSEL. The major airlines generally have at least four available CAROUSELS in the baggage claim area. They are identified by number or letter.

Are there four CAROUSELS because airlines anticipate four flights landing at the same time? No. The four CAROUSELS are there for

PROCEDURE!

Q. What is the meaning of "PROCEDURE"?

A. PROCEDURE is another way of saying, "SCREWED."

Q. Isn't "SCREWED" a rather harsh term? Couldn't a more appropriate word have been used?

A. Yes, but the more appropriate word is even harsher.

PROCEDURE is simply the process which requires that all passengers be made to wait for no less than ten or more than twenty minutes at THE WRONG CAROUSEL.

HOW THEY GET YOU TO THE WRONG CAROUSEL

Who knows why airlines choose to sucker passengers into waiting at the wrong CAROUSEL? Maybe it's their way of lightening up the passenger's day. To the passenger who might scream, "My God, our lives are in the hands of crazy people!" a reasonable response might be, "Come on, where's your sense of humor?"

CAROUSEL misdirection methods are simple and varied. First, of course, the passenger is encouraged to go into the baggage claim area. At this point certain techniques come into play:

1. YOU'RE-ON-YOUR-OWN

You walk into the baggage claim area and there's no one to ask which CAROUSEL will be delivering your baggage. Sometimes your flight number does not appear on any of the CAROUSELS. Sometimes only alien flight numbers appear on all the CAROUSELS. Other times there are no flight numbers posted at all. You're on your own.

2. THE SKYCAP DECEPTION TACTIC

The passenger sees a SKYCAP hurrying by and shouts, "Which CAROUSEL for Flight 128?" The bustling SKYCAP usually answers, "Coming in on krole!" You shout, "What?" He shouts, "Four!" So the passenger waits at CAROUSEL 4, unaware that part of PROCEDURE is misinforming the SKYCAP.

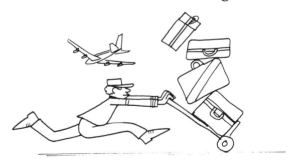

3. OUIJA BOARD

Here the crowd is given substantial wandering latitude in the baggage claim area. Cleverly, airline persons are sent hurrying through with much-too-busy expressions on their faces. You can try to ask, but you'll never get out more than, "Say, can you tell me where. . .?" The POOPING here is rampant and obvious. Eventually the crowd gathers together around a particular CAROUSEL, quite unintentionally, like coming to a conclusion on a OUIJA BOARD, the consequence of an unconsciously cooperative guess.

4. BAIT AND SWITCH

This is the most ingenious method of all. One of the four CAROUSELS is already in motion when you get into the baggage claim area. Or it is put in motion when most of the crowd has gathered. On the moving CAROUSEL is one suitcase; one lone suitcase moving promisingly on its circuit. The offer is too much to resist — this *has* to be the right one! You and two hundred others will stand gazing idiotically at this one bag going round and round, not knowing your baggage will be coming in on another CAROUSEL.

Q. Isn't this slight inconvenience far outweighed by the care and thoughtfulness expended by the airlines in their effort to offer the safe and expeditious delivery to us of our baggage?

A. No.

Q. What is the difference between a major airline and an ordinary airline?

A. A major airline maintains a regular schedule of employees' strikes.

Q. When is it much better to be a woman than a man?

A. When you're in the lavatory and the plane hits turbulence.

WHO CAN YOU KVETCH* TO WHEN YOU'VE BEEN DUMPED ON?

*kvetch — make known one's displeasure, not necessarily in hopes of remedial action, but not exactly expecting indifference.

A FOR-INSTANCE SCENARIO
IN TWO PARTS:

PART I

You're very tired, but a heavy meeting is waiting in Seattle. Thank God it's a two-hour flight. You can get in a good hour-and-a-half snooze. You get to the gate early, get your seat assignment, board a 727 Stretch. You have a problem.

"Yes? May I help you?"

"I hate to bother you when you're boarding passengers, but my seat, it doesn't recline."

"Oh, well that is because you are in a non-reclining seat."

"I know that. When I said my seat doesn't recline what I meant was I'm in a non-reclining seat that doesn't recline."

"Fine. Will you excuse me now? We're awfully busy. If I can help you with anything else just press the call button."

"Right now is when I need the help."

"I'll get back to you as soon as we're airborne."

"That'll be too late. I'll be stuck in a non-reclining seat for the whole flight. Two hours. I was hoping I'd be able to. . ."

"I'm terribly sorry, but there's nothing I can do right now. Did you request a reclining seat?"

"No. I didn't know I had to. I just thought. . ."

"Well, if you didn't request one. . .Will you please excuse me? I really don't have time to talk right now?"

"Please, don't leave me. Who else can I talk to? It's important! I mean, you've got maybe 110, 115 seats on this plane, how many don't recline? Why would a person think of requesting? Why didn't somebody just tell me? Let me talk to somebody. Let me talk to a chief agent or something."

"We're about to take off. You'll have to sit down and fasten your seat belt. You can talk to a Service Representative in Seattle."

"What the hell good will it do me to talk to somebody after we land? I need to snooze NOW, God damn it! This is horseshit!"

"Well, I don't have to listen to that kind of language, sir. If you're going to scream and use abusive language there's nothing I can do. I was just trying to help you. You can talk to a Passenger Rep in Seattle."

"I'm a desperate man! I was counting on a nap! Please! I'll pay scalper's prices! Why didn't somebody just tell me?"

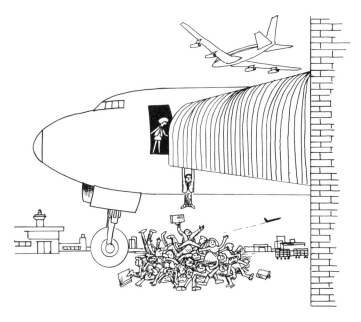

PART II

THE "AREA" ENCOUNTER

Your plane lands. Knowing there's really nothing you can do about what has happened to you, you'd at least like the satisfaction of letting this airline know you've been dumped on and you don't like it. You look up someone in authority.

"How come you don't tell people when they're going to get stuck in a non-reclining seat. It's a rotten, stinky trick!"

"Look, sir, getting upset and yelling isn't going to help anything. If you'll just tell me calmly what the problem is I'll see what I can do."

"There's NOTHING you can do now! That's the point! You people stuck me in a bad seat and I couldn't get anybody to help!"

"Well, I can certainly try. What flight are you on?"

"Off! It's all over. I'm off! Not on, off!"

"Sorry. I misunderstood. But of course if the flight is over...I mean, I'm not sure what I can do for you at this point. But if you've had a problem I can certainly bring it to the attention of the right department. That I promise."

"Now! I want to talk to the right department right now!"

"That would be impossible, sir, our main offices are in Cairo, Illinois. May I see your ticket?...Mm-hm...Mm-hm...Now I see. You see, you came in on a 727 Stretch. That equipment has two seats with limited recline and two seats with no recline."

"Why are you telling me this? Why would I want to know this?"

"Look, I'm just trying to help. I'm trying to find out just what happened. You have a return ticket here and I want to be sure you don't have the same problem going back. Now, which was it you wanted, the limited recline or the non-recline?"

"OH WOW! OH SHIT! OH SHIT SHIT SHIT!"

"All right, if you're going to use that kind of language this conversation is over. I don't have to listen to that."

"I WANTED RECLINE! NOT LIMITED! NOT NON! RECLINE! I NEEDED A NAP!"

"Oh, now I understand. I'm very sorry and I apologize for the incovenience. You have my personal promise you will have a fully reclining seat on the return flight. Please accept my apologies."

"Does it come as a surprise to you that your apologies do not make me feel like I've slept for an hour-and-a-half? Why wasn't I told about the non-reclining seats? Shouldn't people be told?"

"I don't know. To be perfectly frank, this is the first complaint I've ever had about seat recline."

"The first? The very first? I'm the very first complaint?"

"Fourteen years. Thousands of passengers . . ."

"And no one has ever until this day complained about getting a non-reclining seat? I'm the first in your entire life?"

"My sincere apologies. I wish I could do more."

"How come the Flight Attendant was so...?"

"What could she do? Surely you didn't expect her to force another passenger to trade seats with you, did you? Go to another passenger and ask him or her to get out of a reclining seat just so you could go sit in it? Is that what you wanted?"

"Of course not. I just..."

"Well then, with due respect I give up. Just tell me what it is you want me to do. I mean, I've already apologized and assured you I'd report the matter and make sure you have a reclining seat on your return trip. What else would you like me to do?"

"If someone had just told me. I mean, if I knew..."

"No question we were definitely in the wrong there. Let me suggest that next time you request a full recline when you make your seat selection, okay? Avoid problems, right?"

"Am I really the first one to complain about. . . ?"

"Don't think about it."

"I'm sorry."

"No sir. You were the one who was inconvenienced. I'm the one who's sorry. I apologize."

"The language. I was tired, grumpy."

"What the heck. You were upset. Justifiably."

"Convey my apologies to the Flight Attendant. And thanks."

"You're entirely welcome."

The passenger was unquestionably dumped on, but wound up apologizing. How did it work? Read it again. See if you can spot the Airline Rep's more effective guilt lay-ons. Which do you feel were the most effective? The sneakiest? How often in your own life have you run into the "first-complaint routine"? Is this used only by airlines or by other service-oriented businesses as well?

Q. What action can the victim of a airline dump-on take when he or she is told, "Since your inconvenience is already over and done with, and since I've apologized and said I'd report it to the proper department, I really don't know what else you want me to do about it"?

A. Scream and jump up and down.

Q. If you write a letter of complaint to the main office of the offending airline, what will be the result?

A. You will get a courteous apology stressing how much FLYBY AIRWAYS values its passengers and regards their comfort and convenience as paramount. After reading the letter you will feel a lot better if you scream and jump up and down.

Q. Has it ever happened that a plane actually departed at a time like 8:32 a.m.?

A. Yes. Most frequently it happens with planes scheduled to depart at 7:41 a.m.

A few years back airlines began realizing they were hot stuff. They were carrying lots of passengers and lots of baggage and they were getting more and more organized. Yet, despite increasingly advanced procedures, their baggage-misplacement operations were woefully lacking in precision. It was hit or miss.

In airports all over the world misplaced baggage stood in unattended clusters gathering dust, nobody noticing them. Suitcases, garment bags, cardboard cartons — each with its own story to tell — accumulated in baggage claim areas unclaimed, unloved.

One day the airlines got together and said, "Hey, if we're so good at everything else, how come we're so sloppy about losing baggage?" Others, of course, rose to point out that when it came to quantity the airlines had nothing to be ashamed of. This drew applause.

But one fiery young executive dared to speak of neatness. He asked the assembled airline leaders if they were proud of their style. "I, for one, take little pride in being part of an industry which relies on luck rather than technique in the task of baggage misplacement," he shouted. He spoke of planning and care and the good feelings engendered when lost baggage is returned to owners. "How," he demanded, "can we return a lost suitcase if we are not careful to lose it in a recoverable way to begin with?" He added forcefully, "An industry meticulous enough to say something like '4:14' rather than take the easy way and say '4:15' should be meticulous enough to lose baggage in a decent and orderly fashion!" They gave him a standing ovation.

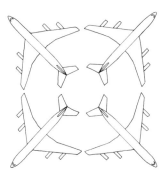

Thus enthused, the airlines formed the famous SYSTEMIZED BAGGAGE SCREW-UP METHODS.

FIGURE #1

Passenger (a) departs in plane (b) as passenger's bag (c) is left in terminal (d).

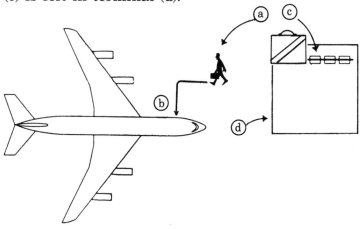

FIGURE #2

Passenger (a) boards plane for Detroit (b) as passenger's bag (c) is put on plane for Sri Lanka (d).

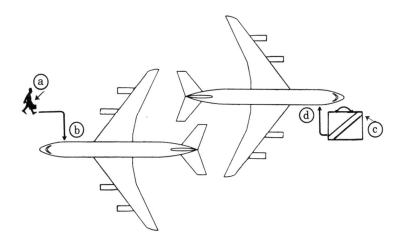

FIGURE #3

Baggage including passenger's bag (a) is unloaded from plane (b) *but this is an intermediate stop* which is why passenger (c) is reboarding plane to continue on to his destination.

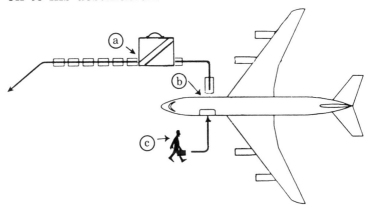

FIGURE #4

Passenger (a) makes change from one plane (b) to other (c) as passenger's bag (d) is taken into terminal (e) where it will be left.

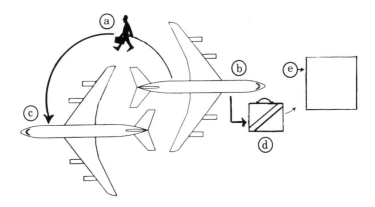

Q. Is the suggestion being made here that airlines deliberately misplace baggage?

A. No. The suggestion being made here is airlines don't deliberately *not* misplace baggage.

As airlines developed more and more sophisticated methods for the misplacing of baggage, they felt a need for the refinement of place. They knew that things, especially big things like suitcases, don't just get lost; they get moved or picked up or put away. They knew that NOTHING JUST GETS LOST — THINGS GET LOST *TO SOMEPLACE.*

And this is why, when your misplaced baggage is returned to you, the airline says, "It somehow got routed to Columbus, Ohio."

Q. Does all lost baggage go to Columbus, Ohio?

A. To the best of our knowledge Columbus is CENTRAL LOSING. Your misplaced bag will go there unless Columbus is where you are going. In this case the airline will say, "It somehow got routed to Tulsa." Or sometimes, but rarely, "Topeka."

Q. What if you're traveling on an airline which doesn't have any flights to Columbus?

A. Don't worry. It will get there anyway.

Nobody is pointing a finger at honest, hard-working baggage handlers. The airlines seeking perfection entrust highly trained and experienced specialists with the delicate task of screwing up a person's trip. Interestingly, the preference in hiring goes to illiterates incapable of reading baggage tags. Equally select are certain health freaks who enjoy lugging heavy bags fifty yards out of the way so they can put it down in the wrong place. These are highly valued specialists we're talking about.

Q. What are these specialists called?

A. Sons of bitches.

Q. Before it actually happens, how can you tell a plane is about to hit turbulence?

A. The Flight Attendant is serving coffee.

"What are you up in the air about?"

"I'm on a short flight, seated in row 23 like I've got something catching. I order a Scotch and I wait and wait. By the time I get my drink and pay for it, the plane is descending and the Flight Attendants are picking up the empties. I yell, 'Hey! Fly in a holding pattern for a few minutes so I can at least take a few sips!' Nobody listens. So I chug-a-lug the whole drink. So, don't ask why I'm up in the air. Ask why I'm walking this way."